DREAMING WITH RED CLOVER

A Plant Spirit Short Read

Heather Sanderson

Majestic Wisdom Publishing

Copyright © 2020 Heather Sanderson

Majestic Wisdom Publishing
www.majesticwisdompublishing.com

All rights reserved.

This book is not intended as a substitute for the medical advice of physicians or psychologists. The reader should regularly consult a physician or psychologist in matters relating to his/her/their health and particularly with respect to any symptoms that may require diagnosis or medical attention.

Cover image by WikiMediaImages under the Pixabay Simplified License on www.pixabay.com. The original image has been cropped.
Editing by Deanna McFadden

ISBN: 9798576590056

CONTENTS

Title Page
Copyright
Introduction	1
Plant Consciousness	4
What is a Plant Spirit?	7
What Does it Mean to Dream with a Plant?	8
How to Dream with Red Clover	10
The Spirit of Red Clover	16
Overview of Red Clover Medicine	20
Red Clover Folklore	23
Journey into the Dream with Red Clover	25
A Bonus Benefit	29
Over to You	31
Acknowledgements	33
About the Author	35
Books by this Author	36

INTRODUCTION

For several years I traveled and lived from place to place with no fixed address eventually moving over one-hundred-and-sixty times. Each time I was ready to move on, I relied on trust and support that places would appear as I needed them. And, generally, they did, giving much to the kindness of both strangers and my own support system, I was never without a place to safely rest my head. Upon returning from my studies in Ireland one time, I stayed with friends in their apartment near Inwood Park, far from any other neighborhood I had lived in before in New York City. One dewy morning, I wandered to the park and felt a nudge to go and sit on a hill covered with Red Clover. While I had learned a bit about Red Clover in various herbal classes and loved drinking infusions of her delicious flowers, I never spent real time with the plant, so I sat.

Having paper and pen with me, I drew her, noticing her green triple leaves with white patterns, her seemingly spikey pink flowerhead and how soft it was to the touch. Another nudge reminded me that

I had a bag of Red Clover dried in my storage unit. I promised the plant that I would take the three-hour round trip from 207th Street down to South Street and back to get them the next day. With that commitment made, Red Clover nodded and set me free to continue with my day.

That same night I spoke with someone who was upset about learning that one of her friends had been diagnosed with breast cancer. She called to ask if I happened to have any Red Clover (who has an affinity for working with breast and womb cancers). Stunned with the realization that this was why I had been told to go and get the plant from storage, I shared with her my morning experience and then asked where her friend lived. As circumstance would have it, she lived two buildings away on the same street where I was living for the week. It felt as though Red Clover had orchestrated it all. From my friends taking me in at this particular time, to the encounter with Red Clover, and being able to help this woman in this way. The next day I delivered the Clover directly where it was needed.

Often dismissed because she is so common, many overlook Red Clover's incredible healing properties and keen ability to orchestrate what needs to happen while offering nourishing support. With a particular association to the Triple Goddess and archetypes of the Maiden/Mother/Crone, Red Clover focuses on aiding the womb through all life stages and helps balance duality or opposing energies. She nudges you to remember the natural flow of energy and will encourage you to ignite, grow, and balance your own inner fire so you can bring your passion into action.

PLANT CONSCIOUSNESS

What does it mean to talk with or connect with plants? More so, why would anyone want to? To work with plants means that you need a foundation of understanding that they are conscious beings. In general, you might think of consciousness as awareness or a field of "something" of which we are all a part. It's that intangible source or energy that helps shape every aspect of our being and behavior.

Once you are able to see a plant as a conscious and living being, you can then understand more of their intelligence. Plants are our ancestors and they have been here on Earth a lot longer than humans. They have evolved physically over a great deal of time in order to adapt and thrive as environmental conditions change. This information is stored in their consciousness, displayed physically in their forms, and in their behavior. Many herbalists and people who work in Sacred Plant Medicine say that plants are so intelligent they know in advance where they will be needed—either medicinally or for another healing purpose—and grow in those places patiently waiting for humans to realize why they're there.

By dreaming with a plant, you are able to access or share in their consciousness, to receive information, and possibly even instruction. Often this has to do with healing spiritually, psychologically, emotionally, or physically—and it can also be more tactile.

When I connect with Red Clover, her guidance and information is a push on my shoulder, a message. She wants me to take physical action, like in the case of going to my storage unit to help her get to where she was needed. She has also pushed me to step into my power with messages of action such as "be your abilities" and by inviting me to "step into the fire others set for you—without fear. Step into the fire —it's the only way." Both of these messages call for direct action and the need to heal the parts of me that feel judgment, resentment, and anger of others and within myself. To no longer let fear of getting burned prevent me from stepping up and into myself or sharing my abilities with others.

The information you receive may not be healing in nature. It may have to do with creating something—a piece of art for example or a different way of living. It could be a direct action that needs to happen. You don't need to work just with Red Clover for this, it can be any plant or tree. For example, I met a magnificent 800-year-old Oak tree in Ireland. After spending some time in her presence, I closed my eyes and asked if there was anything I could do for her. The Oak tree asked me to clean up the trash around her trunk (I heard these words appear out of nowhere and saw an image of her trunk). When I went to do so I found a used diaper that someone had stashed inside a hole in the bottom of her trunk. When removing the diaper, I felt flooded with gratitude at being able to do so. It was something that was so simple to do but I never would have looked there if I hadn't been shown what was needed. You can see with this clear example, any work you do with any plant, whether or not it's Red Clover, is possible and will be beneficial in some way.

People in many cultures, though not all, have forgotten that the plant, animal, and human worlds are not separate. Humans tend to separate and then believe in dominance or power over the other worlds. Again, not all humans do this, I'm speaking generally here and also from experience. When a person enters into the dream (or consciousness) of a plant it is there that the worlds of both become united and equal. It is with attention that we can then start to co-create with the plant world. If you think of the example of the Oak tree and imagine that its consciousness was talking to mine in some way, you can discern that the tree has no arms or legs but could ask me to do something on its behalf. Imagine if all humans were connecting with and listening to plants in this way and what we could achieve together.

WHAT IS A PLANT SPIRIT?

The concept of a plant spirit is difficult to put into words because it can be experienced in so many different ways. To me, plant spirits are the consciousness and essence of a plant—that which is embodied in its physical form and exists around and outside of the physical body as energy and/or vibration. The spirit of a plant may also exist without a physical presence.

Think of your own spirit. What does the word spirit mean for you? Maybe you think of spirit as that energy or quality which animates your body, a vibration in your heart, the part of you that connects to some larger energy or life force. Beyond the energy of the physical plant, the spirit has the ability to move and be moved and to communicate in many ways that we can see, hear, feel or sense in some way, and often ignore. Dreaming with a plant is important because you can gain a sense of connection with what spirit means for you.

WHAT DOES IT MEAN TO DREAM WITH A PLANT?

Dreaming with a plant can mean many things. If you think of when you are asleep and dream that is when you are able to connect with another plane of consciousness without much effort. If you try to remember your nighttime dreams and work with them, there is always information to aid in your healing and wholeness. There is always information that you can bring back from that "other" non-physical world of the dream into your physical world. To dream with a plant means to share in consciousness or that dream place. Instead of entering it passively, as you would when asleep you choose to enter this other world, pay attention to what comes, and then bring information back with you. You might consider this as active imagination or deep listening.

Often this means entering your own dream-state or altered state of consciousness where you can be both awake and asleep. In that dream-state, you are open to receive information in a different way. The rational mind isn't completely gone, but it's not necessarily as vocal as it usually is, and these dream-like qualities can reveal other kinds of information.

Contrary to many beliefs, this does not require any mind-altering or hallucinogenic substances. In my experience this is a natural exchange of energy and information between humans and plants. It's an innate ability that we all have within us (before we learned how to be separate). This might be a challenging concept for some so we'll next talk more specifically about how to enter this dream state, what to do there, and why it's important.

HOW TO DREAM
WITH RED CLOVER

As you develop or deepen your relationship with a plant there are key steps you can take to enter and work in the dream world. Some are concrete and more practical, and others require you to use your imagination and intuition. If you want a relationship with Red Clover, a helpful first step is to go and sit with the physical plant in nature. To do that, you might first need to identify Red Clover and where she grows near you.

Red Clover is native to Europe, Western Asia and Northwest Africa and has made her way to North and South America. She grows in fields, lawns, meadows and roadsides where there is plenty of sunlight. She usually grows to be about four to six inches tall and her stem carries a few clusters of green leaves with a dash of white coloring. The leaves grow in threes. Her flowerhead has a more pinkish hue than red with a white undertone. Red Clover flower looks like a ball comprised of little spikes and often stands taller than other plants around.

Once you have identified Red Clover, or you are called to her intuitively, it's a good practice to ask permission from the plant before any encounter. As you approach you can ask in your mind or with a thought intended for Red Clover, "is it okay for me to sit with you?" Once you feel a sense of "yes," then sit or lay down beside the Red Clover. If you aren't sure what it means to "feel a sense of yes" that's okay—you might hear the word "yes", or get a feeling that all is well, or your head might even start to nod. However your own intuition guides you towards consent.

Once you're seated with the plant you can start to softly study her. Look closely at her stem and leaves. You can gently touch her leaves and feel the texture there. If there is a flower head present, pay attention to how the flower is constructed and look at variations of color. Notice any sensations you feel. You can smell her scent. Red Clover is safe to eat, and you might taste a bit of her leaf or flower. The more sensory organs involved in this meeting the better. This is something that you can take your time with and really get to know the plant. You might consider drawing her to further deepen your connection. This might be your entire encounter and, whether you are aware of it or not, in this exchange you are already working on many levels with Red Clover. The joy of being in company of a plant friend is beneficial for both you and the plant. In my experience, plants tend to like the attention.

If you want to explore other connections with Red Clover, to go deeper into a dream state and into the world of the plants, there are several ways to do so. One way to do this is often called merging but you may hear other names such as entering an altered state of consciousness, shamanic journey, or active imagination. This is where you start to form a connection with the less physical aspects of the plant like her energy, consciousness, or spirit.

Some people like to work with their hands and try to sense the energy field of the plant. With Red Clover, for instance, you might place your hands a few inches away from her and see what you notice. If you have trouble feeling something that's okay and if you don't believe there's anything there, that's okay too. If you try, you might be surprised by what you can feel even if it's invisible to you. If you'd like, you can think of it as a bubble of energy or light around the Red Clover plant like a forcefield or egg to help contain her and keep her healthy. Some people like to see or imagine a little being or energy that lives with the plant and helps her thrive. These beings are sometimes called Elementals or Devas, though they have many names. You can also think of this as an aspect of the energy and/or spirit of the plant as well.

Next, it's often helpful to close your eyes and start to imagine you are Red Clover. You become her. This process is where you merge with the plant. This is where, if you want to, you can think of it as using your active imagination. Here you may experience seeing visions, feeling sensations in your body, hearing sounds, or being moved physically in ways that are unusual for you. It is also possible that nothing much will happen, especially the first time. Using your active imagination is like a muscle and if it feels a bit rusty, keep trying. Plants are extremely patient teachers so there's no pressure to get something right or have it look or be a certain way.

Once you can feel or see yourself as Red Clover, imagine what it's like to be her. Maybe you can feel what her stem feels like as if you're on the inside of it. How does it feel to become a leaf or her flower? What qualities do you notice? What does it feel like to sit in the sun? Imagine what it's like to transform with the seasons or be present with what is happening right now. It's helpful to fill in as many details as possible. It can be useful to draw or write down some notes as well. This might feel like enough and you can do this as often as you and Red Clover want to.

As you merge and imagine, you are going deeper into the dream or consciousness of the plant. You might feel a desire to move, dance, sing, or you might see images or a story. If you are someone who sees images, one way to work with what is coming through from Red Clover is to draw or paint, in an abstract way, whatever you are shown. This is interesting to do as a group. To do this several people sit with Red Clover at a distance from one another not looking at what the others are drawing. Usually, once everyone is finished and shares their work, you will see that common images, themes, and colors have come through. The group's consciousness has joined together and merged with the plant's consciousness—and now you have visual proof. This also helps with confirmation if you feel skeptical or doubtful in any way (plus, it's fun to do!).

As you can see, there are a lot of options to experience connection with the less physical aspects of a plant. Once you have established a connection in a way that works best for you, you can ask a question of Red Clover. Maybe it's a question to do with your life or something you need help with. Perhaps it's a question for her. Whatever it is, hold it in your mind and, staying in a merged state, see what answer comes. It might be an image or word. A sentence or two. Again, you might move or dance or hear sounds. You might feel vibrations that aren't "yours" and discern what it means when you sense another energy. There are only right answers and the more open you are to any perception, the more answers you will receive. It's helpful to write down or record whatever comes.

You can then ask if there's anything Red Clover needs from you. Wait to receive an answer and then, if it's something you can agree to, do so and be sure to follow through with the request. Again, writing it down helps. Asking if there's anything you can do helps keep things reciprocal and helps restore an even balance of power between plant and human worlds.

Lastly, give thanks in some way—by expressing gratitude or giving an offering of some sort. This might be a physical offering like a bit of lavender, cornmeal, or another plant that wants to be offered, or it could be a song or dance. Some way of giving back and giving thanks for all that has been shared.

Once you feel complete, it's important to return fully from this experiential place. To come back from this journey or dream you deepen your breath, place your hands on the earth and move your body. Bending your knees if you're standing helps to stay connected and also brings you back to everyday awareness.

THE SPIRIT OF
RED CLOVER

Now that you've explored merging with Red Clover, let's look at some of her attributes and what they might indicate on a psychological or spiritual level. These may be different than your own personal encounters and that's okay because your information and intuition is what matters most.

Red Clover embraces the nature of duality, helps find balance and comfort within, and reminds us that things may not always be as they seem. You can see this in her nature. For example, though her appearance looks like fire, she is sweet and cooling to drink. She gives the impression that she's sharp and spiky when you look at her flower and is actually soft to the touch. With these qualities in mind, she can help you remember that situations, interactions, and beliefs you hold about yourself or others, may not be what you think. She urges you to move out of the mind and into your emotions. That way you can feel your way through life and not be quick to judge or form opinions.

Red Clover champions duality and honing your ability to merge aspects of yourself that seem to be opposite. This manifests in ways like bringing your masculine and feminine energies into balance, merging opposing emotions like joy and sadness, or listening to someone who holds a belief different to yours. Even polarities like anxiety and depression share qualities and are often ways that the same energy tries to emerge. Red Clover reminds us that there is no "other" or separation and works in the nature of inclusivity so that you can incorporate all aspects of self, including the parts that you might not want to acknowledge. This in and of itself is healing. When you heal and find this balance within yourself you can allow others to be themselves creating inclusivity in the world around you.

With her leaves growing in threes Red Clover works with the energy of the Triple Goddess to weave together all aspects of life. This connection to the Triple Goddess is a nod to Red Clover's sense of divine orchestration or creating alignment to get things done. The Triple Goddess has many faces like the Celtic Goddess Brigid who embodies the archetypal energy and real-life phases of The Maiden, The Mother, and The Crone. The Triple Goddess's energy works in a spiral. While a woman might move through these phases in her lifetime chronologically, the shape reminds us that you consist of each of these parts of life, no matter your age or gender. Nothing is linear. You can be the Maiden and the Mother and the Crone and step in and out of these roles depending on a situation or what you need.

The spiral also builds on the concept that nothing fully exists or can grow in the opposing nature of either/or. Either/or sets you up for an endless cycle of attack and internal stopping points. For example, "either I am a Good Person or a Bad Person" because of what I have done or will do or won't do. Instead Red Clover asks that you see life in terms of and/and. When you step into the and/and nature of being, these absolutes of "Good" and "Bad" (or any other fixed notions of black and white) have no place. You can accept that you have qualities that you are comfortable with and areas you might want to grow. The more you step into an and/and mindset the more opportunity there is for growth and acceptance and you can then embrace more of your many gifts to bring into the world.

Red Clover's association with fire and the sun helps to activate your own inner flame or to help balance excess heat. This fire could mean anger, passion, sexual energy, transformation or any other quality you associate with fire. She helps you to stand in your true power, burn away beliefs that prevent you from doing so, and to learn how having heart paves the way for ultimate power. When you merge the opposing forces within you, and operate in a balanced way, the judgment of others (or feeling of their unbalanced power being cast upon you) has no weight. When you have balanced fire, powerlessness also burns away, and there is no need to compare yourself to what others may have accomplished or have in their lives. Red Clover protects you so that you can dismantle the energy of criticism and instead focus on bringing your abilities into service.

OVERVIEW OF RED CLOVER MEDICINE

Red Clover can be ingested as a tea or infusion by steeping dried leaves and flowers in boiled water for at least twenty minutes before straining. She also works well as a tincture by placing the leaves and flowers in alcohol for 4-6 weeks then straining. A standard tincture dosage is about 30-60 drops in a cup or so of water. As a tonic, Red Clover brings nourishment and support to many systems of the body as she's rich in vitamins, particularly C and B, and a whole host of minerals including magnesium, zinc, copper, selenium and calcium. Her medicine has a particular affinity as a treatment for preventing or working with cancer cells (particularly breast and ovarian cancer) and in healing the womb.

This work with the womb is where you can again see her association to the Triple Goddess and the Maiden/Mother/Crone archetype as she helps in all phases of womanhood. For a young woman she brings nourishing support that the body needs more of when menstruating to offer a healthy period and flow. Red Clover helps to strengthen, thin and purify the blood. This is part of why she is associated with menstruation, and these are not the only benefits of her actions. She helps blood to flow optimally through your circulatory system and creates nutrient rich blood for a healthy lining of the uterine wall in case of conception. Supporting the blood in these ways helps your body run more efficiently without blocks and aids in the release when menstruating. With this power comes knowledge that since Red Clover thins the blood it is not advisable to ingest her before surgery or if you are already on a similar medication.

When entering the Mother archetype, she helps bring a balance to the acid/alkaline levels in the vagina and uterus which can help foster a fertile womb that is inviting to sperm and conception and in this way can help with infertility. Even if you have no plans of birthing a child, have had surgery to remove your uterus, or don't identify with these cycles in your body, Red Clover awakens the Mother energy within you so that you can give more of that energy to yourself or others.

As a body enters into the Crone time of life and menopause, Red Clover has the ability to boost estrogen, help you move through hot flashes, and aid in osteopetrosis. If you are already on hormone pills or estrogen replacement therapies, it's best to avoid Red Clover. In each phase, Red Clover strives to bring comfort and balance through significant changes in all stages. Like a divine cloak, Red Clover embodies the energy of a protectress and guide, keeping those who move through these cycles safe at times when they are vulnerable physically, energetically, and spiritually.

RED CLOVER FOLKLORE

In addition to the Triple Goddess, Red Clover's three leaves is also associated with the Holy Trinity of The Father, The Son and the Holy Spirit. This association as well as the Triple Goddess calls to mind the overall cycle of Birth/Life/Death and that all things rise, fall and are born again. Thinking in threes also moves away from duality and indicates that there is always a third binding spiritual non-physical force or "other" with you right from conception. The way that Red Clover holds both the triple Christian masculine principles as well as the feminine Triple Goddess indicates that she does help balance these both within you. She can help you not to get caught up in beliefs of holding only one way or the other as true, and helps with this balance in a larger way for collective consciousness.

Perhaps because of her strong association with the Holy Trinity and Triple Goddess and her strong nutritive qualities, Red Clover holds a value of protection. Popular belief shows that as far back as the Middle Ages people used Red Clover as a protective floor wash or poured her on an area to clear out unwanted spirits and energies and to cleanse space. You can add her to a smudge to let the smoke do this work or carry her with you to ask for protection.

Along with protection all types of clover are associated with luck, especially if you happen to find a four-leaf clover. Some say the luck comes if you pick it and others if you leave it be. This particular kind of luck you might associate with extreme good fortune or the "luck of the Irish" and leprechauns and perhaps that's not far off as Red Clovers are known as Fairy Flowers. To see a field of Red Clover means that you can enter the Fairy World and by tasting a flower or asking for entry you might get access to this other realm. The leaves can also protect you on this journey into the Land of the Fae or Fairies and help you return fully to your body afterwards. Keep that in mind when you go on a journey with this powerful plant.

JOURNEY INTO THE DREAM WITH RED CLOVER

Another way to work with the spirit of Red Clover is to call on her wherever you are, even if you aren't physically sitting with the plant. Her energy and consciousness are everywhere, and you can dream with her, feel her presence, or ask for her help, wherever you are. To aid in this, let's take a guided journey with Red Clover and see what happens.

You might want to take a few moments before reading on to center yourself. If you'd like to, find a comfortable way to sit or lay down. Close your eyes if that feels safe or let them be soft. Take a few breaths and allow yourself to feel your body around the breath. When you feel at ease, open your eyes and read this bedtime story with a soft dreamy feeling.

❖ ❖ ❖

You're cozy in your bed, about to go to sleep, when you see a glowing green door appear in front of you.

As you move toward the door, it opens, and you step through to find yourself standing in a field beside a dark forest. See the dark trunks of the trees, the thick pine needles and leaves overhead, and notice the dim light inside the forest. You are on a quest to find a magic flower that will bring healing.

Take as long as you need to imagine this place.

There's an opening into the forest in front of you and you slowly enter. The path is unclear and you intuitively know where to go. You walk deeper and deeper into the forest, seeking the magical flower.

There is a soft light ahead and you walk towards it to arrive in a small clearing surrounded by a circle of trees. The darkness is illuminated by a bright pink flower with three petals. You see the energy of the flower as a pulsing light. The flower expands and contracts as does the light. Notice this energy and how you feel.

The flower begins to grow with each pulse, and it opens. You tumble into the flower, head first. You are inside the flower and traveling through it, surrounded by dark pink. It feels like a slide or a tunnel you move through. As you move through this tunnel you move backward through time. Move backwards through your life.

See moments when you felt happy. Moments when you felt sad. Moments of anger. Moments of calm. Take your time, there's no rush. Rest on each moment that appears as you travel backward through your life.

Your journey continues and shows you moments of support. Moments where you felt shame. Moments of loss. Moments of celebration.

Take yourself all the way back to before you were born.

Find yourself in the womb. Feel the energy of your mother. The energy of her mother. What circumstances brought you here? Known and unknown. Whatever they may be, feel what this knowledge feels like in your body.

Ask yourself what you will bring into this world. See the answer. If no answer comes, that's okay. Hold yourself with love. Rest in your love.

You feel a familiar pulsing. Expansion and contraction and you start to move back through the tunnel. As you slide through the tunnel this time your life plays forward from any point. See only moments of love.

There is a moment where everything pauses. Pause here and see the gifts and abilities you want to bring into the world. See them clearly. What are you already doing? What might you want to grow?

When you feel ready, you emerge from the flower and return to the forest. The flower glows more brightly and you thank her for the medicine you have received. There are glimmering lights floating in the forest now. You follow the lights like a path back through the forest. Walk all the way back to the edge where you began, and you see the glowing green door. You open the door, step through, and come back into your body. Come back into your breath and back into yourself.

◆ ◆ ◆

Once you are back fully from this dreamy journey, you might write down feelings that emerged, the gifts and abilities you want to bring into the world, or moments of love, or drift off to continue dreaming in some way.

A BONUS BENEFIT

One of the most valuable parts of any practice where you are working with plants and in the world of consciousness is developing trust. You might be someone to discount or not trust in your own intuition. Likely because of messages you have received from a culture that holds value in beliefs of power, dominance, and separation and/or early childhood messaging that was reinforced over time. For example, if you were open to the plants as a kid, an adult who was already closed off may have told you that your experience was invalid or not real. While this was not true, someone you may have loved or who was in a position of authority dismissed your experience. This messaging often damages your relationship to your own intuition and eventually causes an imbalance when it comes to trusting your instincts (especially when it comes to psychic awareness or abilities).

Beginning the process of being with and merging with plants and their world helps to heal this split. In time, and with repetition, it can help you reconnect to your own psychic and spiritual gifts and Self. This, in turn, can empower you to feel more whole, connected, and become able to make more decisions from a place of safety and trust in yourself. As you continue to grow in these ways, you can go into a dream-like space or vast field of consciousness and bring back visions, dreams, or instruction on what to do in this physical realm of your daily life and personal growth.

OVER TO YOU

Some may say that plant spirit healing works on the psychological level because we are able to see a mirror into ourselves through them. Others call it intuition or a psychic awareness and receive all kinds of different information. Whatever words work for you, there is no harm in seeing what might come from connecting with a plant. You can even ask to see what would be for the greater good of all, if that helps. The most important thing is that you find your own direct relationship with Red Clover and discover for yourself what you can give to one another.

You were called to this short book for some reason. Whether it was to know more about plant spirit medicine, Red Clover, listening to spirit or divine orchestration, working to find balance of the masculine and feminine energies (and other dualities) within, to find your abilities, or for some other reason, perhaps unknown, Red Clover called you here with her magic. Now you are equipped to venture out and travel between worlds, dream with

Red Clover, and see what transformation comes. Transformation and healing aren't always easy and may not feel comfortable at times but with a strong ally like Red Clover and your own intuition and guidance I hope you will continue to explore your relationship with her and with the plant world.

ACKNOWLEDGEMENTS

First, I'd like to thank my dear friend and editor, Deanna McFadden, for her constant support, curiosity, and skillful editorial hand. While writing this book I reflected fondly on my first experience with merging in general, led by Susan Grimaldi at the New England Women's Herbal Conference. This was followed by a Shamanic Weed Walk with Susun Weed where she helped participants be with and merge with plants. Since then I have also worked with Elyse Pomeranz who brought in the option of painting or drawing with the consciousness of the plants and am so grateful to have completed a three-year apprenticeship in Sacred Plant Medicine with Carole Guyett in Ireland where I learned to go even deeper into the dream. Each of these teachers has taught me how to enter the plant world and to walk between that world, the dream world, and our human one. To understand that they aren't separate but feed one another and need tending. It is from this place of deep gratitude that I wish to now share these practices with you in my own voice and way. Of course, with the deepest respect and love for the plants who are guiding it all.

ABOUT THE AUTHOR

Heather Sanderson has been working with plant spirits her whole life. In 2013 she studied herbal medicine at Third Root in Brooklyn, NY which led her to a 3-year Sacred Plant Medicine Apprenticeship with Carole Guyett in County Clare, Ireland. It was through this training, and several initiations with plants, that she became immersed in the dream and consciousness of the plant world and found a passion to share it with others. For more information visit www.journeythroughyoga.com.

BOOKS BY THIS AUTHOR

Plant Spirit Short Reads
Dreaming with Dandelion
Dreaming with Elder
Dreaming with Heather
Dreaming with Holly
Dreaming with Goldenrod
Dreaming with Lavender
Dreaming with Nettle
Dreaming with Red Clover
Dreaming with Rhubarb
Dreaming with Rosemary
Dreaming with Sumac
Dreaming with Sunflower
Dreaming with Trillium
Dreaming with Violet

Tree Spirit Short Reads
Dreaming with Apple
Dreaming with Birch
Dreaming with Hawthorn
Dreaming with Oak
Dreaming with Redwood
Dreaming with Spruce
Dreaming with Willow

Healing Arts Short Reads
Loving Kindness for Everyday Life
Understanding Reiki
Yoga Nidra for Everyday Life

Poetry
Sister, (a collection of poems)

The Future is Possible Series
Building the Future Now Through Reiki: A Conversation with Nathalie Biermanns
Building the Future Now Through Yoga: A Conversation with Deanna Green
Creative Being: A Conversation with Gérome Barry
Envisioning New Ecosystems: A Conversation with Stewart Hoyt
Holding Space to Heal: A Conversation with Holly Ramey
Nature Sanctuary for the Future: A Conversation with Marina Levitina
What Art Can Do: A Conversation with Janet Morgan

Visit www.majesticwisdompublishing.com to learn more.

Made in the USA
Columbia, SC
02 December 2024